For Everything
There Is a Season

For Everything There Is a Season

A Book of Meditations for Single Adults

Compiled by
KAREN GREENWALDT

UPPER
ROOM BOOKS

NASHVILLE

For Everything There Is a Season

Scripture quotations not otherwise identified are from the Revised Standard Version of the Bible, copyrighted 1946, 1952, and © 1971 by the Division of Christian Education, National Council of Churches of Christ in America, and are used by permission.

Scripture quotations designated TEV are from the *Good News Bible, The Bible in Today's English Version,* copyright by American Bible Society 1966, 1971, © 1976, and are used by permission.

Scripture quotations designated JB are from *The Jerusalem Bible,* copyright © by Darton, Longman & Todd, Ltd., and Doubleday & Company, Inc. Used by permission of the publishers.

Scripture quotations designated NJB are taken from *The New Jerusalem Bible,* published and copyright © 1985 by Darton, Longman & Todd, Ltd. and Doubleday, a division of Bantam, Doubleday, Dell Publishing Group, Inc. Reprinted by permission of the publishers.

Book Design: Jim Bateman
Cover Design: W. Paul Proctor
First Printing: November 1988 (5)
Second Printing: May 1989 (5)
Library of Congress Catalog Card Number: 88-050240
ISBN: 0-8358-0586-7

Printed in the United States of America

*For everything there is a season, and a time for every
    matter under heaven:
a time to be born, and a time to die;
a time to plant, and a time to pluck up what is
    planted;
a time to kill, and a time to heal;
a time to break down, and a time to build up;
a time to weep, and a time to laugh;
a time to mourn, and a time to dance;
a time to cast away stones, and a time to gather stones
    together;
a time to embrace, and a time to refrain from embrac-
    ing;
a time to seek, and a time to lose;
a time to keep, and a time to cast away;
a time to rend, and a time to sew;
a time to keep silence, and a time to speak;
a time to love, and a time to hate;
a time for war, and a time for peace.*

—Ecclesiastes 3:1-8

Contents

Contents

Foreword

by Susan A. Muto

Single voices are voices of pain and promise, sadness and solace, loneliness and love. They echo the human condition with its deep valleys and heights of vision. This is a book that listens to the full range of dissonance and harmony with which men and women speak of what matters most in their lives: a sense of calling, a need for companionship, a purposeful profession, a place of honor in a vast and at times uncaring cosmos, an intimate relationship with Christ.

It is in the end this sense of being befriended by God, of being God's friend, that redeems single persons from the danger of superficial, self-indulgent living, often accompanied by a sense of loneliness that weighs heavy on the soul and prevents the passage from being alone to feeling at one with

---

Dr. Muto, a single Catholic laywoman, is executive director of The Epiphany Association, a center for adult Christian formation located in Pittsburgh, and an adjunct professor of classical spiritual literature at the Institute of Formative Spirituality at Duquesne University. She is the author of numerous books and articles, including Celebrating the Single Life.

9

others and God in joyful solitude and generous solidarity.

As this book makes amply clear, single life offers countless opportunities for respectful, supportive encounters. We are less likely to feel lonely when we are with other persons, giving that extra inch or mile. These moments of befriending pull us out of the trap of self-pity. Being present to others, stopping to listen to their troubles, complimenting them for being thoughtful or accomplishing their task well—such outgoing acts enable us to transcend the loneliness of single living and to grow in the art of befriending others with the kind of love that finds its source in God.

Whenever I find myself becoming harsh, rigid, full of complaints, and uncharitable, I know I am harboring a negative spirit. Nothing is more harmful to singles than this spirit of negativity. It attracts to itself ill spirits, like hardness of heart, that may be etched into harsh facial lines; pettiness spilling over into cheap gossip; resentment that crops up in envy of another's creativity; lack of forgiveness that harbors feelings of displeasure toward another, to say nothing of maladies like pervasive fatigue, sickly self-pity, and depressive moods. A black cloud hangs over one's single life, and people rightly regard such a person as a killjoy.

This unloving spirit is always divisive. It thrives on gossip and gripes. Underneath all of the misery, we learn from this book that there still lurks a soul longing for the peace and joy of Christ. Our gracious God has the power to dispel this spirit of negativity, to soften the mark of harshness, to give us the grace we need to prevail over evil and the darkness it breeds.

Instead of ignoring others or stepping over or on them, with the Lord's help, we may be able to open our hearts to all in charity, compassion, and commitment. These formative dispositions enable us to renew our intention to love God and neighbor while welcoming the daily detachment that will gradually purify our hearts and promote communion with Christ.

If we want a vivid illustration of what it means to love warmly yet freely, we can meditate on the life of Jesus. As a single person, he had about him an ease, graciousness, and affection that could draw all hearts. He touched responsive chords in whoever met him, sharing with them wonder and joy as well as grief and weariness. He could thrill to the appeal of nature and be delighted by the innocence of a child.

Many writers in this book are witnesses to the art of Christ-like loving. They love as full-blooded, enfleshed women and men who run the risk of loving as Christ did. Jesus does not want us to develop a counterfeit love of formal politeness, impersonal tolerance, or vague humanitarianism. Rather he wants us to root our love in the earthy reality of our humanness while struggling to imitate the example he gives. Like Christ, we must listen first to the will of God speaking in the deepest recesses of our hearts and, out of this listening, hear and respond to the pleas of his people. Then we find the fulfillment that comes from being fully alive single persons, who live in joyful obedience to the divine word, to the message we never tire of hearing:

"What I command you is to love one another" (John 15:17, JB).

Introduction

What is a meditation book for single adults? It is a book filled with the thoughts and feelings of adults who are single by choice or circumstance;

—a book that describes growing and changing understandings of and relationships with God;

—a book in which the reader can find belonging, challenge, pain, despair, joy, peace, and hope;

—a book through which the reader can consider relationships with friends, family, and strangers.

This book reflects the life of a single person in our society, with all the attending emotions, conflicts, decisions, and responses. The authors represent single adults of all ages, interests, vocations, and stages of life. Their words address their own feelings, their understandings of singleness, and their relationships with God and with others.

As I read the vast number of poems and prose pieces submitted for publication, I found myself drawn into the experiences of these authors. Their words and images challenge and provoke, support and strengthen, nudge and encourage. I discovered wholeness and healing in their ideas and insights.

These authors risk sharing their inner thoughts and emotions. That risk becomes a gift to us, their readers, as we learn what it means to live in relationship with God and others. To the reader, in whatever circumstances of joy or sorrow, these authors give comfort, strength, and hope in claiming the words of Ecclesiastes 3:1: "For everything there is a season, and a time for every matter under heaven."

Through these words and images, readers are connected not just to the authors but also to the countless number of single adults across our world. In fact, these words and images connect us to the singleness of every individual—those places where we all stand alone before God, ourselves, and our neighbors. These authors challenge us carefully to touch those parts of ourselves so that we might acknowledge and then struggle with who we are and who we can become. Through these meditations, we are all united to the world of single adults and beyond that to all persons around the globe.

Each chapter in this book is composed of meditations, scriptures, poems, and questions to set the tone of the chapter. Individuals can spend a week or more if necessary with each chapter. Allow the verses, thoughts, and feelings of the authors to connect with your own deepest self. The questions for reflection will help your own feelings come into focus. Use these contributions as inspiration to express your thoughts and feelings in writing.

Members of Bible study and prayer groups can use this book in similar ways. During group times, select one or more of the scriptures for study. Members can share the meditation, poem, and/or scripture that meant the most to them and explain why they experienced meaning. Share original writings.

On a personal note, I want to thank Kathi Breazeale Finnell for creative and helpful additions to this book. Because of her efforts, we have a much fuller and more useable book of meditations.

Karen Greenwaldt

"A Time to Break Down, and a Time to Build Up"

Loneliness

How long, O Lord? Wilt thou forget me for ever?
  How long wilt thou hide thy face from me?
How long must I bear pain in my soul,
  and have sorrow in my heart all the day?
How long shall my enemy be exalted over me?

Consider and answer me, O Lord my God;
  lighten my eyes, lest I sleep the sleep of death;
lest my enemy say, "I have prevailed over him";
  lest my foes rejoice because I am shaken.

But I have trusted in thy steadfast love;
  my heart shall rejoice in thy salvation.
I will sing to the Lord,
  because he has dealt bountifully with me.

—Psalm 13

Empty Spaces

Sometimes there's a loneliness
(   )
(   )
(   )
Even God can't fill.

Asa Sparks
Alabama

Setting the Tone

1. Am I making time for rest and renewal to build up myself? If not, what changes could I make in my life?

   a. List possible changes on paper. Place a star next to the most important ones for you.

   b. Commit yourself to practice your selected changes.

2. Am I living in a self-made box? If so, what are the benefits?

3. What would it take for me to venture out of my own darkness and fully embrace life?

4. Will I trust God to guide me in embracing unknown parts of me in my darkness?

A Parable

Once a young woman lived in a box. It was really a very ordinary box. What the young woman liked best about the box was its darkness. She wrapped the darkness about her like a velvety new blanket. It calmed and comforted her. It made her feel safe.

Inside the box, the young woman enjoyed listening to the noise, laughter, and singing of others outside the box. Sometimes, she even put her ear up to the side of the box so she could hear them more clearly. After they went away, she would imitate their singing and laughter, but somehow, one person singing or laughing alone didn't sound the same as several people singing and laughing together.

They kept calling to her. The young woman went over to the side of the box and listened for awhile. Then she took her fingernail and very carefully made a small indentation in the side of the box. She listened some more. Then, using her fingernail like a drill, she made a very small hole in the box. She peeked through the little hole.

She saw all of them outside. They were laughing and singing and having fun. The young woman thought about how much she would like to join them. But, then she thought to herself, *What if I go out to join them and they don't like me? What if they throw stones at me, or gang up on me, or push me? What if they kill me?*

Motivated by these frightening thoughts, the young woman retreated to her favorite corner and sat down. She felt tired and sad. Suddenly, a tiny beam of light came through the small hole she had made and penetrated the darkness. It glistened and shone like a fragile, radiant thread, connecting her with the outside world.

The young woman stared at the light. Quietly, she snuggled into the corner and hugged the blanket of darkness around her.

Sharonn Davis Halderman
Pennsylvania

What Color Is Loneliness?

What color is
  loneliness?
Is it misty gray
  nothingness
    or drab brown
      dullness?
Is it cold shades of blue
  that chill empty spaces
    of the heart?
Is it sharp black and white
  of harsh judgements
    that shut you out?

No.
  Loneliness is
    golden yellow,
      laughing orange,
        joyous red . . .
          all the bright colors
            of sunshine and warmth,
              a kaleidoscope
                of happiness
                  placed
                    just
                      beyond
                        reach.

Glenda Taylor Emigh
Pennsylvania

20

Turn thou to me and be gracious to me;
   for I am lonely and afflicted.
Relieve the troubles of my heart,
   and bring me out of my distresses.
Consider my affliction and my trouble,
   and forgive all my sins.

Consider how many are my foes,
   and with what violent hatred they hate me.
Oh guard my life, and deliver me;
   let me not be put to shame, for I take refuge in thee.
May integrity and uprightness preserve me,
   for I wait for thee.

—Psalm 25:16-21

When you pass through the waters I will be with
      you;
   and through the rivers, they shall not overwhelm
      you;
when you walk through fire you shall not be
      burned,
   and the flame shall not consume you.
For I am the Lord your God, the Holy One of Israel,
      your Savior.

—Isaiah 43:2-3

Loneliness

Loneliness is something within . . . a deeper feeling that can occur whether we are by ourselves or in a crowd. It is a need for a sense of oneness in spirit, a sense of belonging and sharing of ideas, feelings, and sometimes even physical presence. There are moments when the best way to combat loneliness is to run, keep busy, until we can sit alone and deal with the feelings. Sometimes delaying dealing with loneliness is wise. Of course, such delays can tempt us to keep running in order never to deal with the feelings. Then again, there is the danger of the opposite happening—staying alone too much for fear of reaching out or sharing ourselves with others.

Perhaps the pain of loneliness makes us need the comfort of the supreme being that tells us we are not alone. In quiet moments of listening or even in the loudness of a crowd, we can find the presence of God. Knowing that God is present makes me know that I can be by myself. Through God's presence, I realize the need to maintain a healthy balance between aloneness and being with others. Through this presence, I have been able to deal with myself and those moments of loneliness. Also through this presence, I can learn that I really am not alone. God is there, as are friends and family. In the silence of aloneness, I can learn how to reach out to those who are near.

Listen and wait. Do not be afraid to be with that inner self. Know that the awesome presence of God can be your survival. Touch that loneliness deep within and ask God to help you reach out . . . to be yourself in order to be with others.

Jeanetta B. Benedict
Virginia

Alone

Each day I walk
Through the desert
Of broken relationships,
Remembering bits and pieces
Of love
Which, in fleeting moments
Of happiness,
Promised
A bright and happy future.

Alone,
I walk among the crowd
Wondering
If there may be
One as lonely as I
Aching to hold
And be held,
Capable of enduring
Love.

Lord,
My heart is made
For loving and being loved.
I feel the comfort
Of your loving arms
And pray
That some day
Arms of flesh and blood
Will enfold me
With gentle care.

Bonnie Elizabeth Taylor
Oklahoma

My Creation

There's a lot of lonely people in the world,
    And I suppose I've made some of them that way,
By rejecting them,
    by shunning them,
        by ignoring them,
            by not giving them enough of my time.
There are too many important things to do.
Then, when I get lonely, I ache
    Because no one has time for me.
If I help to create a lonely world,
    I must face the fact that one day I will live in it.

W. Scott Davis
South Carolina

The Opening

Alone, O Lord, alone with thee,
Where none could speak nor hear nor see,
The bar I've placed across my heart
I'd lift, and bid the doors to part—
On rusty hinges open wide
And let just once your love inside;
And when I'd turn to close the door
And put the bar in place once more,
My heart so filled with thee I'd find
The doors could not be closed behind.

Shirley Gupton Lynn
Tennessee

Soul Cry

O Great Source of Life,
Why did you create me
And put me here—amidst many, all alone?

O Great Giver of Peace,
Why did you choose me to be
An ambassador of your love to others?

O Great God of All,
I have felt your mark upon me,
I have struggled in darkness with fear,
I have questioned with audacity your wisdom,
And now I am empty!

In my emptiness, I come to you.
In my aloneness, I seek your presence.
In my fear, I ask your consolation.
In my weakness, I need your strength.

Recreate me, O Lord,
That I might fulfill that calling
Which you have placed upon me.
Calm me, O Lord, that I might
Be filled with your peace.

Amen.

Sharonn Davis Halderman
Pennsylvania

When Jesus spoke to the people again, he said:
I am the light of the world;
anyone who follows me will not be walking in the dark
but will have the light of life.

—*John 8:12 (NJB)*

Dear God,

This passage in Ecclesiastes is painful for me to read. Tears of sorrow well up with the acknowledgment that there is a time to refrain from embracing. How I have ached to feel the warmth and security of being hugged and held. Slowly I am coming to realize that I must spend periods of time alone with myself and with you to discover unknown parts of me hidden in darkness. It is through these times that I grow toward wholeness by embracing these newly recognized parts of myself. With this new knowledge, I am able to offer more of myself. Thus I am able to embrace more fully another.

O God! Help me celebrate the times *both* to embrace and to refrain from embracing.

Amen.

Kathi Breazeale Finnell
California

"A Time to Weep, and a Time to Laugh"
Celebrating Singleness

See to it that no one makes a prey of you by philosophy and empty deceit, according to human tradition, according to the elemental spirits of the universe, and not according to Christ. For in him the whole fulness of deity dwells bodily, and you have come to fulness of life in him, who is the head of all rule and authority.

—Colossians 2:8-10

Being Single in a Married World

God has not created any half people. The idea we are half people until we are married is a misunderstanding of the creation story. Some people seem to think God created Eve because God had to complete the half person, Adam, whom God had already created. Reading the creation story, we realize God made Eve because Adam was alone. Despite all the animals God had given Adam, he was still lonely. Adam needed company, not completion.

Frederick G. Cain
Indiana

Setting the Tone

1. What are the sources of brokenness and separation in my life?

2. What are the sources of connection and wholeness?

3. What are specific ways I can affirm and celebrate my own singleness?

4. How should I assess my growth as a child of God?

Room for Me

Is there room in your church for me?
I'm a divorcee.
I tried so hard to hold it together.
But I could not.
And now he is gone.
To your women I am a threat
Of publicly perfect marriages.
To some of your men
I am a desperately available body.
To God I am a soul
Seeking worship and help.
Is there room in your church?
For me?

Asa Sparks
Alabama

Society's Eyes

Always watching
Always wondering
Why—A single
Inquiry continues
Single forever
My choice

Kay Frances Kizer
Missouri

Being Happily Single

I am convinced that being happily single is like being happily married. It takes time and work. To be happily single, one accepts the unique joys and sorrows of singleness. Being happily single is learning to live in the now. Being married is good, not better. Singleness is different, not less fulfilling. When we accept this truth, we can live in the now and rejoice in today's gifts and challenges.

In addition, singles have two responsibilities: to accept the biological or adopted family and to create a family of friends. The family and friends that have been with us for years are still there for us to enjoy and be with. We need to let these people be just who they have always been—sources of love and support. We also need to create a family of friends. That means reaching out and risking the development of friends where we are now.

If we are to be happily single, we have to accept and enjoy the reality of our sexuality. As we seek to live as sexual beings, we need to find ways to express our sexuality that do not compromise our faith or our value systems.

As single adults, we are first and always a part of God's family. Remembering this, we will know that Christ can be the source of hope and joy for singles as well as for the rest of creation. This hope comes from the God we know through Christ and who encourages us through the scriptures. In our baptism, we have all been affirmed as God's children. As children, we receive the gifts of God's Spirit—the gifts of "love, joy, peace, patience, kindness, goodness, faithfulness, gentleness, self-control" (Gal. 5:23). The gift of self-control supported by the other gifts of God's Spirit can and will keep us full of the joy of being single while still living with its sorrows. The gift of God's Spirit affirms us now and enables us to risk being in family, to risk being happily single. This gift of God's Spirit can and will give us patience with our church, with ourselves, and with our neighbors as we all struggle to accept the affirmation of God's love that is ours in Jesus the Christ.

And so, my single friend, "I remind you to rekindle the gift of God . . . for God did not give us a spirit of timidity but a spirit of power and love and self control" (2 Tim. 1:6-7).

Hazel Alene Winterburn
Wisconsin

Enemy

I'm trying to win a friend, Lord . . .
   someone hard to please,
     demanding,
     unbending,
     critical,
     and unforgiving.

She showers
  understanding,
  compassion,
  and acceptance
    on everyone but me.

She cheers the stranger
  with a smile,
  encourages acquaintances
    with kind words,
     and nails my transgressions to the wall!

She hurts me
  and is afraid to love me.
    Help me, Lord,
     to be a friend
      to myself.

Glenda Taylor Emigh
Pennsylvania

One Voice

In the chorus of trees
we enter alone,
walk through alone and die alone.
Touching is a gift
like dew in the forest
and as each love fades,
we grow from ashes.
Buds sting in the birth
on any tree.
Each leaf one,
each leaf separate;
the breeze touches all sides
like insight that allows change.

Ann Zoller
Oklahoma

On Being Alone

It is curious that, growing up in the society of other human beings, we learn to make certain assumptions about the reality we inhabit. We have something like a tacit agreement among people to accept such ideas without regard to whether or not they accurately represent the truth about human existence. The idea that a person's sense of well-being and self-worth is dependent upon circumstances is one such assumption. We assume, for example, that people who have physical handicaps, who are chronically ill or disabled, or who have family members so afflicted are unhappy. Or we tend to believe that the poverty-stricken among us are discontented, despite our platitudes about riches being insufficient to bestow happiness.

Another generally accepted notion is the assumption that the natural condition of every adult is to exist in a state of matrimony, or at least some quasi-matrimonial relationship. It is taken for granted that all single people, like water rushing to the lowest level, are intent upon getting married. Those who demonstrate an inability to find mates are objects of pity. Those who do not aspire to be married are thought to be, at best, eccentric or, at worst, worthy only of scorn and suspicion. Although western civilization is less constraining in this regard than other societies, still the unmarried are made to feel that their singleness is unnatural. In many ways, unmarried people are non-persons. And, whether single by choice or happenstance, people who are alone are naturally expected to be lonely. After all, outward circumstances surely determine one's inner state of being.

The apostle Paul, however, discovered something

about human existence that challenges these commonly held assumptions of ours. "I have learned," he wrote in his letter to the Philippians, "in whatever state I am, to be content" (4:11). Paul's life is testimony that our inner state of being is not a function of the outward conditions of our lives. We are faced with the possibility of being content whatever our circumstances or, perhaps to be more accurate, despite those circumstances.

It is worth noting that when Paul writes about being "content," he is not commending to us a passive acceptance of the world as we find it. The Greek word that Paul uses and which is often translated as *content* or *satisfied* means "being suffcient and adequate in one's self." What Paul seems to be talking about is maintaining a sense of self-worth in the face of the conditions of one's existence. This special ability to be content is very like what the theologian, Paul Tillich, calls the "courage to be." He defines that as "an ethical act in which man affirms his own being in spite of those elements of his existence which conflict with his essential self-affirmation."

Could it be that being alone does not necessarily mean being lonely? Perhaps being alone requires only courage. This courage would affirm the value and worth of human life regardless of the circumstances in which that life unfolds and in spite of our assumptions about happiness and marriage.

Meanwhile, we must admit that marriage has a prominent place in the Bible. Besides being a sacred institution, marriage is frequently used to describe the relationship between God and humankind. This metaphoric use of marriage not only helps us understand God but also casts the marital relationship between a man and a woman in a new light. The faithful can treasure this concept of marriage and use the notion of God's "marriage" to Israel or Christ's betrothal to his church as a way of illuminating their earthly marriages. Being single, however, is illuminated as well by the unity, the oneness, and the standing-apart of God.

Though God is, in a very real sense, alone, God is not lonely. God lacks nothing. God is sufficient and adequate. God does not know the desolation or bleakness to which we mortals are prone. God does not exist in any set of circumstances, social or natural.

As human beings, however, we do exist within a world and within situations that are often not of our own choosing. We are given to a certain sense of emptiness in the absence of other human beings. And yet, none of this need determine who and what we are. We also are capable of courage, of affirming ourselves in spite of the conditions in which we live. We can be alone without being lonely—not because we are adequate in ourselves as God is but rather for the very opposite reason. When we are alone before God, our very weakness serves to create an opening between us and God. When we enter into a relationship with God, our very being is affirmed by God.

So, not only can our aloneness be a sign of our individuality and our standing apart from all other individuals in our unique places in creation, but our aloneness before God is also a basis for a relationship with the source of our being. Might we, either married or single, then, learn to be content in our aloneness? Might we not have the courage to be alone without being lonely?

Lawrence Beaston
Pennsylvania

Everyday Living

I feel separate and independent—
Making my own decisions,
Thinking my own thoughts,
Doing what I want to do—
And being a little scared
Of being separate and independent.

Helen G. Hopkins
Pennsylvania

Alone—Never

Single—yes
God gave a bird
God gave a tree
God gave a flower
God gave an animal
This I share
With all creation
Alone—no

Kay Frances Kizer
Missouri

What man of you, having a hundred sheep, if he has lost one of them, does not leave the ninety-nine in the wilderness, and go after the one which is lost, until he finds it? And when he has found it, he lays it on his shoulders, rejoicing. And when he comes home, he calls together his friends and his neighbors, saying to them, "Rejoice with me, for I have found my sheep which was lost." Just so, I tell you, there will be more joy in heaven over one sinner who repents than over ninety-nine righteous persons who need no repentance.

Or what woman, having ten silver coins, if she loses one coin, does not light a lamp and sweep the house and seek diligently until she finds it? And when she has found it, she calls together her friends and neighbors, saying "Rejoice with me, for I have the coin which I had lost." Just so, I tell you, there is joy before the angels of God over one sinner who repents.

There was a man who had two sons; and the younger of them said to his father, "Father, give me the share of property that falls to me." And he divided his living between them. Not many days later, the younger son gathered all he had and took his journey into a far country, and there he squandered his property in loose living. And when he had spent everything, a great famine arose in that country, and he began to be in want. So he went and joined himself to one of the citizens of that country, who sent him into his fields to feed swine. And he would gladly have fed on the pods that the swine ate; and no one gave him anything. But when he came to himself he said, "How many of my father's hired servants have bread enough and to spare, but I perish here with hunger! I will arise and go to my father, and I will say to him, 'Father, I have sinned against heaven and before you; I am no longer worthy to be called your son; treat me as one of your hired servants.'" And he arose and came to his father. But while he was yet at a distance, his father saw him and had compassion, and ran and embraced him and kissed him. And the son said to him, "Father, I have sinned against heaven and before you; I am no longer worthy to be called your son." But the father said to his servants, "Bring quickly the best robe, and put it on him; and put a ring on his hand, and shoes on his feet; and bring the fatted calf and kill it, and let us eat and make merry; for this my son was dead, and is alive again; he was lost, and is found." And they began to make merry.

Now his elder son was in the field; and as he came and drew near to the house, he heard music and dancing. And he called one of the servants and asked what this meant. And he said to him, "Your brother has come, and your father has killed the fatted calf, because he has received him safe and sound." But he was angry and refused to go in. His father came out and entreated him, but he answered his father, "Lo, these many years I have served you, and I never disobeyed your command; yet you never gave me a kid, that I might make merry with my friends. But when this son of yours came, who has devoured your living with harlots, you killed for him the fatted calf!" And he said to him, "Son, you are always with me, and all that is mine is yours. It was fitting to make merry and be glad, for this your brother was dead, and is alive; he was lost, and is found."

—Luke 15:3-32

Curtain Time

"All the world's a stage and all men and women
merely players . . ."

Why do I feel I've missed an important cue?
  Where is the prompter
    To feed me my lines?
I look around me
  at all the other players
    and see confidence,
      self-assurance,
        happiness,
          and success.

Am I the only one
  without a copy
    of the script?

Glenda Taylor Emigh
Pennsylvania

Think about

Moving Forward

Strange little moments.
September heat unrelenting.
Random thoughts about
Christmas.
Saturday garage sales.
Bought
My own Christmas tree.
Guess
The subconscious knows
I am here
To stay.

Asa Sparks
Alabama

Acceptance

Labels

In some ways, "single" is a label given to me by those who are married. It is a means of identifying and proclaiming difference. As such, it can divide me from those with whom I would be united. With a few exceptions, I do not do much with married people my own age because their activities are all designated for couples. They tell me I would not feel comfortable.

Once I can accept the label "single," I can get past it. Once I stop categorizing people by whether they have a ring on their finger, I can begin to know them as people. Single is part of who and what I am here and now, but so is my shoe size. It makes me different than those who are married, but it need not separate me unless I allow it to do so. In accepting and living with my singleness as an attribute, I affirm that part of my wholeness and better share my wholeness with others.

Marilyn R. Pukkila
Maine

Conviction and Choice

Everywhere she goes, people make subtle remarks reminding her that at twenty-eight she has passed the age of marriageability, which is a tragedy if not a sin. Tomiko is attractive, has a quick wit, and thoroughly enjoys life. Being a believer in Jesus by conviction and single by choice, she has totally devoted her spare time to serving the one-hundred-member congregation with which she worships.

The church in Tokyo is her source of life—her *family*, she calls it. This family is of utmost value. Her own kin have all but ostracized her for the double fault of being Christian and single. The church is deliberate in supporting Tomiko and other single women in a society that can be extremely cruel to them.

What an inspiration and witness Tomiko is to other singles in one of the world's largest cities. She "bears her cross" of the ridicule rampant in her society, finding her strength in God, in a caring, supportive congregation and in ministering to the world in which she finds herself.

Bill Roy
Alaska

Insight

When I was a child
I used to cut gingerbread people
With a funny cookie cutter
And I observed as I decorated them
With raisins and cinnamon dots, they were all the
    same.
And—in childish innocence—
I assumed that the sameness of puffy gingerbread
    people
Somehow spoke to me regarding
The shape of humankind.
But, as I have grown,
I have learned slowly and painfully
That my earlier observation was not only untrue,
But unnecessarily confining.
I have learned that people, unlike gingerbread
    cookies,
Speak to me of individuality and uniqueness.
Yet, as I ponder this discovery,
I sense that there is somehow an underlying
    design
An elusive thread—common to persons in the
    midst of their diversity.
And, possibly it is this unsung harmony in
    humanity
For which we yearn.
Perhaps we need to recognize that our common
    design
Emerges and takes on substance,
Only as we learn to celebrate
That which is unique within each of us.

Sharonn Davis Halderman
Pennsylvania

Two Trees

I saw a beautiful tree yesterday. God, it was magnificent to see. A tall straight trunk, limbs that reached out, and broad, fleshy leaves that seemed to beckon the passersby. As people passed, they stopped and gasped and admired its beauty. Yet despite its awesome appearance, the tree was fragile. Nurtured by the best possible soil, watered gently by loving hands, sheltered from the wind by a large plastic dome, the tree was fragile and tragic. The tree was made beautiful by an environment that made it unable to grow beyond a protective covering.

I saw another tree today, God. Its snarled trunk twisted its way upward. Twigs and branches lying broken at its feet showed it had been watered by torrid rains and winds. Beside the branches rested last year's leaves, crumbled and dead, mysteriously transformed into the soil that will nourish this year's growth. The tree stood alone in quiet solitude. No one looked at it, for where it stood was cold. The wind whipped hard, and the snow covered its feet with a hard, crusted coldness. The tree was very strong, yet it too had its tragedy. That which made it strong also made it alone.

I am these two trees. I have been pampered in the perfect environment of loving parents, happy childhood, and a strong faith. This environment produced an easy-going personality, a winsome smile, and easy achievement often admired by others. This perfect environment also produced the appearance of weakness and insensitivity to the hurts and pains of the world.

Another side of me has grown in deep silence, nourished by broken dreams that I never shared, tears that never fell down my face, inner doubts that came out as faith statements, hurt of a broken marriage, and hundreds of other quiet, painful struggles shared only to you in prayer. This side of me is strong and can face any battle, yet its very strength is what makes me alone.

My struggle, O God, is to make these two one. I do not want the world to turn my joyful smile into grim determination, nor do I want my pain to be pampered into weakness. Help me, God, to make one tree, beautiful and strong, not sheltered and not alone.

Amen.

Doug Morphis
Kansas

Accepting Singleness

In our couple-oriented society, it's often hard to walk the path alone. It takes a big dose of self-esteem to say, "I'm happy, I'm whole, and it's okay that it's just me you see." Everywhere one turns in the world, traveling, dining out, going to parks or the movies, there are couples. Why do we, as singles, feel so threatened, so lonely, so unwhole because we're alone? It's taken me a couple of years to overcome those feelings. I've had to keep in mind that many couples aren't happy, don't communicate, and stay together only for financial or emotional reasons. I'd rather be alone than be a partner in an unsatisfying relationship. A lot of my inner strength and peace comes from that belief. We have to learn to love ourselves and develop a life-style that we enjoy and find rewarding. That should be the prime goal in life, not the all-consuming quest for a mate. Marriage might happen, and it might not. I have several friends who cling to their partner rather than face the consequences of being alone. I'm proud because I've handled it alone: finances, maintaining a home, working full time, raising two children—things I never believed I could do! It's hard work, but I have a deep satisfaction that I can take care of myself. I believe that God and I can handle whatever comes along in life. I've learned the hard way that one has to find areas of support as a single person. I certainly did. I was lost in a whirl of depression and self-pity until I knew it was time to go into the world and find support. For me it was (and is) a singles group that meets every Monday night. I've found the friendship and caring there that I needed. We whole-heartedly plan discussion groups, outings, and retreats, and we share life's good and bad moments.

It's been an essential ingredient in my being able to smile and say, "I'm single, and I enjoy me and my life."

Marilyn Coleman
New York

After he had dismissed the crowds, he went up on the mountain by himself to pray. When evening came, he was there alone.

—Matthew 14:23

Creator God,

You have made me, and in that making, you called me "good." Sometimes I struggle with who I am—particularly when I become envious of a coupled society. At other times, I burst with joy because of the freedom I feel. Sometimes that joy borders on having a feeling of gloating as I compare my life to that of others. Help me, dear God, to walk carefully between the feelings of struggle and self-satisfaction. Give me a sense of joy that is balanced with concern and empathy for others. *And* most of all, God, provide me with a sense of your presence as I experience these ranges of feelings and thoughts.

Amen.

Karen Greenwaldt
Tennessee

"A Time to Embrace, and a Time to Refrain from Embracing"

Family and Friends

You shall love the Lord your God with all your heart, and with all your soul, and with all your mind. This is the great and first commandment. And a second is like it, You shall love your neighbor as yourself.

—Matthew 22:37-39

Broken/Unbroken

They call our home "broken,"
I don't like that.
We're not perfect, but we love each other.
We struggle to be family to one another.
We laugh and fight and pout and make up
    just like other households.
A wise man once told me, from the perspective of
    twenty years of marriage to the same woman,
"You can be from a broken home with everyone still
    living under the same roof."
So, don't just assume that our home is a broken one.
By God's grace, wholeness comes in a variety of
    packages.

Sandra Mosley Gerhardt
Alabama

Setting the Tone

1. What in my life do I need to let go or let "die"? Am I clinging to something that is preventing my growth?

2. What do I need to embrace to experience new birth?

3. Will I have to share my own pain and suffering as a source of healing for others?

4. What sources of strength can I utilize to overcome my resistance to experience "abundant life"?

Surviving

It's another week until payday. I had to save a couple of this month's bills until next payday because there wasn't enough to cover them. Then three more bills came that I'd forgotten about!

I had just enough food for the meals I'd planned this week, but the kids raided the refrigerator after school and ate what we were going to cook for dinner. My checkbook balance is $2.37.

It's been six months since I've received a child-support check. School's almost out, and I haven't made vacation arrangements for the kids yet because there's not enough money to pay a sitter. At ages six and eight, I can't leave them alone. They don't want to visit their dad, and I don't want to send them. However, I insist on a visit with their dad because, financially, there's no other alternative.

Survival! Sometimes I wonder if I'll make it through another day, let alone another week or month. I mean, I've never been rich, but this is ridiculous! What did I ever do to deserve this? I didn't even want our marriage to end, so why do *I* have to suffer so much? And what about the kids? They've been used to a comfortable lifestyle with a few luxuries here and there. Now we're living in government housing and wondering where our next meal will come from.

Trying literally to survive from one day or week to the next becomes almost unbearable. Dreams are shattered; hope is destroyed. Joy is replaced by the pressure of existence. It's almost impossible to see the light at the end of the tunnel because there are too many obstacles on the path.

Survival! I went through the humiliation of accepting Christmas baskets, food stamps, and Medicaid. I lived in government housing for eight months. There were many days when I didn't know if I had the energy to go on. But, I did go on, and I survived. While I don't have all the answers, I'd like to share some of the things that helped me, with the prayer that they might help someone else.

When making purchases, it's extremely important to distinguish between "wants" and "needs." If things are tight, eliminate all extras and establish priorities on needs. Try to avoid charging things.

Be creative in treating yourself and your family. A friend who was going through rough times felt it was important to treat herself to something special once a week. She set a limit of $1.00 and challenged herself to find new ways of treating herself on that small amount. She went to various restaurants for pie and water, got an ice cream cone at the mall, or bought $1.00 worth of fresh cashews or chocolate fudge. Just as important, she had moments of retreat when she could meditate in order to see Christ in the people around her and in her life. Involve the children in planning for "treats," challenge each other to come up with free activities such as picnics in the park and going to libraries, museums, or concerts. Read the papers and listen to public service announcements for unlimited opportunities.

There are countless books and magazine articles with tips on saving money. Spend some time at the library finding ideas that you can use. Here are some miscellaneous suggestions that I've practiced over the years:

- Make a list of what you need, and don't buy anything that's not on the list.
- Stock up on items when they're on sale.
- Read the ads and plan meals around what's on special.

- Don't go to every store in town to get specials unless you'll be in the area anyway. You'll spend more on gas than you'll save.
- Go to the grocery with a full stomach. It's easier to resist all the temptations if you're not hungry.
- Save on utilities by closing drapes to the sun in the summer and opening them for solar heat in the winter. Get used to cooler thermostat settings (66-68 degrees) in the winter, and higher (78-80 degrees) in the summer. Don't forget to turn lights off when you leave a room, use cold water for laundry, and cook in crockpots.
- Learn to do things for yourself: pump your own gas; fix minor plumbing problems; get a friend to help you change your car's oil. Build your self-esteem and patience in such ventures. Ask questions and learn how to do things for yourself.
- Try the barter system. Trade your skills or talents for someone else's skills. Possibilities include painting, wallpapering, baking, caring for plants, babysitting, or car-washing.
- Don't be too proud to accept help when you need it. Let family and friends give you a shoulder to cry on, an ear to listen, money to pay a bill, an encouraging word, a home to live in.

Live one day at a time. Worry and fear about the future will consume you if you let them. You can become so busy worrying about how to solve tomorrow's problems that you miss possibilities for today's solutions. Find something good in each day. Look for rainbows in the storms, and remember that God has not abandoned you. God will provide the strength you need to make it through any crisis.

Grow spiritually. A strong faith in a loving God

who provides divine support and love can be the difference between survival and defeat. Trust the Lord to provide your needs. I began tithing even when "on paper" I knew I couldn't make ends meet. Amazingly, unexpected money arrived at critical times, reductions in estimated expenditures occurred, and I became content with having needs met rather than with keeping up with the rest of the world. Pray for your former spouse or others who have hurt you and forgive them. Ask God to replace the bitterness and anger in your heart with love, joy, and peace. Thank God for being with you through all the trials to this point, and pray that survival can be replaced with contentment, compassion, and peace.

Rita E. Yackley
North Carolina

"That He Gave His Only Son"

How quickly we remember,

How glibly we recite: "God loved the world so
much that he gave his only
Son, so that everyone who
believes in him may not
die but have eternal life."

We know the agony of Jesus' surrender,

We read his prayer: "Father . . . if you will, take
this cup of suffering away
from me."

We remember his words: "The sorrow in my heart
is so great that it almost
crushes me."

We remember Luke's words: "In great anguish he
prayed even more
fervently; his sweat
was like drops of
blood falling to the
ground."

We can understand how Jesus felt.

But God, how did you feel?

   We see his pain, what was yours?

Did you feel like I felt when she took our daughter
away?

   She whose birth I watched,
      Whose newborn body I held and marveled at
      as life and breath filled her,
      whose diapers I changed,
      whose body I bathed.

She who has grown into a beautiful five year old.

She who fills my house with laughter and joy,
   who loves to play,
      to be read to,
         to go out to dinner, even if it is only "a plain
         hamburger, fries
            and drink."
Now she is gone.
Her laughter no longer bounces off the walls,
The sound of her footsteps no longer floats down
   the hall,
The sound of silence is an agonizing roar,
The emptiness in my house and heart is painful
   beyond compare.
Was it like that for you when you gave your only
   Son?

All scripture in this poem is TEV.

Wayne R. Schaub
Washington

On Thankfulness

I seldom take the time to share my feelings about
you.
  Somehow they get crowded out by the little
  things
    that fill my days.

When I spot the look of joy in your eyes as we meet,
  I'm thankful that in spite of the many weaknesses
    I know about myself
    You find a reason to still be glad about seeing
      me.

When you put your arms around me and hold me
close,
  I'm thankful that neither of us possesses an inhi-
    bition
  That would keep us from using a hug
  To say far more than any words could ever tell.

When I see tears in your eyes because we're parting,
  I'm thankful that we share a common feeling
  About our need for one another.

And when I see you again, dear friend,
And get caught up in telling you about the little
  things that fill my days,
Please notice my eyes and arms.
What they say is far more important.

David G. Broadbent
Florida

"Good Morning, God"

Christ said we should come as little children.

When we see little children and how trusting they are with their parents and how dependent they are for everything, we can truly see what Jesus meant. They come to parents for love, for advice, with expressions of joy, and with hurts and sorrows. So should we go to Christ.

My four-year-old grandson told me he talked to God. After hearing this so many times, I asked him if he heard a voice when God spoke to him. He replied, "Oh no—God just speaks to me in my heart." So, too, should we open our hearts to hear God speak.

My grandson often talked to God in my presence. I tried to capture him in a photo in one such conversation. He just started his breakfast and said, "Good morning, God."

Oh that we might learn to greet each day with such an enthusiastic "Good morning, God!"

Ruth Noble Dearmore
Kansas

Joy in Living

Hugs are
   for children and
   childlike adults.

Hugs express
   joy
   love
   silent laughter.

Hugs are an embracing of life,
   holding it close to the heart,

Yet letting the joy and laughter overflow
   into the world of others.

Helen G. Hopkins
Pennsylvania

Let love be genuine; hate what is evil, hold fast to what is good; love one another with brotherly affection; outdo one another in showing honor.

—Romans 12:9-10

Anger

White-hot, crackling, powerful.
Potentially dangerous.
Knee-jerk reaction.
Honesty. Hard honesty.

The trick is to let your anger loose, but stay in
    control of it.
Walk it, as it were, upon a leash.
Cushion anger between words of caring:
"I love you *and* I get angry with you when (fill in the
    blank) *and*
I'm telling you this because I love you."

And when someone I care about is angry with me,
    what?
Raised hackles, defensive stance, tightened jaw
    muscles, lashing
out to wound deeper? Or perhaps uncontrollable
    tears,
stark terror, churning stomach, a quick escape.
    What???

Lord, would it be strange if we prayed that you teach
us how to be angry with one another? Would you
think us a bit weird and disrespectful for asking that
you show us how to fight lovingly? Can anger pro-
duce a creative spark between two of your children
that contains energy and life and strength and that
can be harnessed for your purposes? If so, our Father,
please show us how. Amen.

Sandra Mosley Gerhardt
Alabama

Day That Will Not End

O day that will not end
   I need a Friend,
      Someone to laugh with,
        talk with.

The hours are long.
   The time hangs in the air.
     Where is the voice,
       the touch,
       the care?

Day that will not end
   Help me,
   Lead me
      To myself.

That there I can find
      The Friend.

Hazel Alene Winterburn
Wisconsin

If I Can

If I can touch your
   troubled mind
And caress it with gentle thoughts,
Or wipe the darkness from
   your eyes
And fill them with sunshine.
If I can lift the burdens from
   your shoulders
And cover them with lace,
Or calm the angry seas of
   your heart
And sweeten the bitter brine.
If I can bring a smile to
   your face
And a dimple to your cheeks,
Or bring a little happiness to
   your life
Then contentment will be mine.

Bill Parker
Ohio

Heavy Burden?

"Lo, I am with you always, to the close of the age."

—*Matthew 25:20*

What is your burden? I know it's very heavy—I can tell from the look on your face and the way that you walk. May I help you carry it today?

You seemed surprised that I would offer. Perhaps we can talk a little as we walk here side-by-side.

I understand that it's not easy being alone with life's burdens. You see, I'm alone, too. I feel the same loneliness, fear, and frustration that come with being alone after having shared life with another.

You thought I had no burden. Oh yes—but I have someone helping me carry mine. Sometimes I take it all back to carry myself, and it gets very heavy. Other times it's given back to me because I take the help for granted and fail to be thankful. Today is a good day and my load is light, so I can help you with yours.

Have you noticed how blue the sky is today? This road has some rough spots, but if we stick to the well-traveled center, we'll encounter less loose gravel. Look! Way ahead—those wild roses beside the road. Have you ever seen such a beautiful color? There's a cool spring ahead where we can stop for a refreshing drink. You'll enjoy the watercress growing there.

My, how quickly the time has passed and how much faster we're walking. There's a fork ahead in the road, and I must turn there. I'm glad to see you smiling and walking so briskly and straight. We've helped each other today, and our loads are lighter.

See that person just beyond the fork in the road? Maybe you can catch up and help with her load. It seems to be quite heavy. I'm sure I'll find someone to help, or, if my load becomes heavy, someone will help me. Remember—stick to the center of the road and keep your eyes ahead, observing the beauty all around.

Ruth Noble Dearmore
Kansas

Communion

Sharing
A cup of tea with you
Is like a holy sacrament.
You bless the vessels.
You bless the brew.
For your tea
You pour your love,
Filling my cup to the brim!
I hold it here like a chalice.
It warms my hand, my cheek, my heart.
Whether we use the moss-green mugs,
Or the small rose-covered cups,
Having tea with you is a sacrament of love.

Pixie Koestline Hammond
California

Friendship

Why do you love me?
What do you see
Within me
That I cannot see?

Don't you see
The pride,
The impatience,
The selfishness?

Can't you see
The superior me?
Irritable,
Aggressive, arrogant?

When I look through your eyes,
I see a caring, inarticulate, sensitive me,
One who listens, shares,
Believes in you.

You've seen both "me's"
And have blended the images
Together to form
The picture of a friend.

Helen G. Hopkins
Pennsylvania

On Friendship

When a friendship survives many years
   A lot of things go unsaid.
Like the times when I've needed so much
   for someone to hear me out
   and simply listen to my confusion.
And, as always, you were there—
   allowing me to ramble
   until the world and all its pressures
   made sense.

Or the times when you came to me
   to share a bit of your sorrow or joy
   when for a moment you could turn to me.
How good it felt to be needed,
   if only for just a while!

And if, for whatever reason,
   we find we don't need each other,
   I pray that we will remember
   that there was a time when we did.
And a time when we might.

David G. Broadbent
Florida

A Favorite Old Sweater

Our friendship fits like a favorite old sweater.

Surrounding me with a soothing warmth,
   I can recapture past emotions with less pain.

Enfolding me with familiar charm,
   I can enjoy the present with a lighter heart.

Being versatile like our changing moods,
   I can wear it loosely over my shoulders or fasten
                                                    every
                                                    button.

Enduring the future with mending and tender care,
   I can depend on its lasting shelter.

Cynthia Heidelberg
Nebraska

Keepsake

Sometimes I hold onto a shirt
   like I do people.
I keep it even when it's become
   worn and faded from the world.
And when someone says why
   don't you throw that rag away,
I simply smile and say . . .
      My friend there's beauty
         in this shirt that you
         will never see,
      And I'll never throw it away,
         it means too much to me.

Bill Parker
Ohio

Facade

Try as I may
There are times when I can't
  bring your face to focus
Except for fleeting glimpses
  in rare moments.

Rare moments for me
Because I've seen little of you
  in any posture,
But some of you in moments
  reserved for special friends,
At special times.

You cry with me for a love I have
  to leave,
You laugh with me with memories
  of outrageous times
  that tempered with love
  and soul-exchanging
  seemed like exquisite normalcy.

You feel with me with touches
  that cause an almost
  imperceptible gasp,
And waft the mind into
Timelessness.

You speak with me, softly,
  and describe your depth
  for that moment,
  in stark honesty.

You rage controllably with
    remembered hurts,
And promise swift retribution
    if ever scarred again.

These changing faces, with
    soft kisses and whispered
    desires,
Overshadow an everyday,
    have-to-keep-living face
That I struggle to keep in focus.

Bill Knuth
West Virginia

Yahweh, who can find a home in your tent,
who can dwell on your holy mountain?

Whoever lives blamelessly,
who acts uprightly,
who speaks the truth from the heart,
who keeps the tongue under control,

who does not wrong a comrade,
who casts no discredit on a neighbour,
who looks with scorn on the vile,
but honours those who fear Yahweh,

who stands by an oath at any cost,
who asks no interest on loans,
who takes no bribe to harm the innocent.
No one who so acts can ever be shaken.

—Psalm 15 (NJB)

Hello God,
   You really are a friend to me—more friend and more family than anyone else. Sometimes I take you for granted or try to replace you with others whom I can see and touch. I rely on them before I think of relying on you. Why do I do that? Remind me when I forget. Create in me a desire for you that cannot be quenched. In your presence, let me find rest and strength for living with people near and far.

In Jesus' name,
Amen.

Karen Greenwaldt
Tennessee

"A Time to Seek,
and a Time to Lose"

Mourning and Memories

O Lord, rebuke me not in thy anger,
 nor chasten me in thy wrath.
Be gracious to me, O Lord, for I am languishing;
 O Lord, heal me, for my bones are troubled.
My soul also is sorely troubled.
 But thou, O Lord—how long?
Turn, O Lord, save my life;
 deliver me for the sake of thy steadfast love.
For in death there is no remembrance of thee;
 in Sheol who can give thee praise?
I am weary with my moaning;
 every night I flood my bed with tears;
I drench my couch with my weeping.
My eye wastes away because of grief,
 it grows weak because of all my foes.
Depart from me, all you workers of evil;
 for the Lord has heard the sound of my weeping.
The Lord has heard my supplication;
 the Lord accepts my prayer.

—Psalm 6:1-9

Memories of Men and Cologne

A scene of sunshine streaming through stained glass on Sunday finds me in church, searching to be uplifted. A new beginning every week. What difference does a new week mean to me? I had lived—no, I had existed for two years of new weeks, 104 new weeks, and the time hadn't evaporated the pain I still felt.

Concentrate, my mind shouts! Concentrate on what Reverend Charles is saying: "Be everything you can be." I wish I could be all that I had been before the divorce. *Listen,* a voice whispers in my mind, *you must forget your past and present emotions.*

Stop! These emotions are making me feel flushed and warm even though the air conditioner is keeping me cool and comfortable on this hot and humid June morning. But as the air blows, it sends whiffs of deodorant soap and a man's cologne that invade my senses. My thoughts are all confused as these scents trigger a remembrance of my former husband's cologne. I not only remember his cologne but also the pungent perfume of the other woman. This new aroma begins a roller coaster of emotions, and my mind cries to be released from this torment.

Think of something pleasant, anything pleasant, insists my inner voice.

These thoughts tumble on and mesh together to remind me of my grandmother Edith, the ever-present bustling human dynamo, who brought stability and love by giving it unconditionally. She took me on long rides for the famous pork barbecues at a local drive-in near Cheat Lake. She was my dad's mother. I loved her dearly, and I know she loved me. She always devoted her life to men: her husband, her sons, my husband, and my son. She always said she just loved "pretty men." She waited on them hand and foot, even to the extent of fixing them a full dinner of crisp fried chicken, fluffy mashed potatoes, pan-browned gravy, and country-style green beans at midnight.

After my grandfather died, she seemed very lonely. He had been ill with an unknown ailment most of my life. He was almost a nonentity to me, and I could not understand what she could miss. She missed having someone alive standing and sleeping beside her. At times she'd have some of the grandchildren stay over for company. We'd all sleep together in the big feather bed, sing and laugh, and have a great time.

The strangest thing, I thought, was that my grandmother wore cologne, Grandfather's cologne. She missed him, and it was her way of being close to him, remembering their good times.

Until recently, I didn't understand how the senses come to haunt you when you long for someone to be close who no longer is. It's taken her death and my divorce, the two most painful events of my life, brought together by the smell of a man's cologne and soap, to understand events that happened twenty-four years apart. The senses are strange phenomena that mesh memories together in my mind and heart.

As the organ plays, the people file out of church; a calming touch, accompanied by a faint smell of a man's cologne, brings me back to reality. A caring voice said, "Donna, are you OK?" My answer reflects more than I realize. "Yes, I just might be."

Donna Love Musa
West Virginia

Setting the Tone

1. What can I do to process my grief?

2. How might my grief be transformed? What new mission is God calling me to accept?

3. As the meditation on page 91 affirms, anger is a part of the grieving process. To facilitate the process, take a sheet of paper and write your responses to these questions:

   a. *Acknowledge:* Do I truly know it is all right to be angry? How can I feel and express my anger in healthy ways?

   b. *Forgive:* Have I forgiven those with whom I am angry, especially myself?

   c. *Release:* How will I utilize the suggestions given in the last paragraph of the meditation to release my anger?

The Sound of Silence

Old books on dusty shelves,
the photograph of one who died,
silent piano keys waiting
for fingers that once played,

these have an eloquence
that does not need a voice,
A sound heard only
by a listening heart.

Doris Kerr Henke
Arizona

In Mourning

I am mourning for my marriage.

Its death was swift and shocking.
Its death was not foreseen.

If only I had felt the symptoms of its illness.
If only I had found a cure for its killing disease.

Looking back won't bring my marriage to life.
As in death, its end is final.

Cynthia Heidelberg
Nebraska

On Leaving

It's a time like this—when you have to
say goodbye—that I'm reminded of my
pact never to get this close again.
But then, someone like you comes along,
allows me to become involved, to care—
to share a bit of your life—shows
such concern and warmth to me; and I
grab it and thrill in being a part of you.

And then you have to leave.

And it hurts so bad. It's like a section
of my being, a part of my heart
taken away. It feels as though my very
breath has left me.

Thank you for caring. Thank you for sharing.
What I am, what I shall do, who I shall be
will be a part of what you have helped to make me.

I know that often my thoughts will turn to you.
But only when I miss the ones
who cared
who shared
who loved—along my way.

David G. Broadbent
Florida

Love Not Returned

The small hospital room smelled like illicit tobacco smoke, sweat, and institutional antiseptic struggling to be noticed. A friend, waiting for a new heart procedure to be tried in lieu of surgery, grabbed my hand as I got up to leave.

"Look, Rick, whatever happens, I mean, if I can't be with Sue Ann and the kids, will you look after them?"

I sat back down, and we talked some more. He had been so sure of the procedure, but now? We talked of death, and he said that whatever was down the road, he would rest easier knowing that someone would be there to look after his wife and two young children. I told him I would.

Three months later, his wife and I tried to talk over the clamor of the children. Her husband was gone. He was not dead but absent by choice, having left on his own. He left with his oldest child asking questions about Daddy and his wife struggling to pick up the pieces.

That was about two years ago. That particular visit and those for the next six to eight months frightened me. A vibrant, intelligent, caring woman punished herself for the total destruction of a marriage that she only half-owned. Her weight fell dramatically. She smiled less each time I saw her and began to blame herself not only for the breakup of her marriage but for the terrible life she feared the children would know with only a part-time father and a mother who could not give them all the time and energy she wanted.

There can only be pain when the statistics on divorce hit home. In that pain, the love of God is real, not in a magical "maybe I'll wake up tomorrow and it will all be over" kind of way, but in a strengthening that helps people get through the pain and learn, endure, and love.

Indeed, just the physical, legal, and financial mountains to climb are great for a person already terribly involved in grieving a lost marriage. The overwhelming quality of those first few months cannot adequately be put into words. That is good, for it would frighten me to think that we could honestly describe such pain. To describe it would mean that in some way we could rationally explain it. But nights spent staring at the ceiling, days lost trying to concentrate on work instead of life, children not understanding but trying to survive themselves in a world that has altered radically—these things go beyond rational description. They go deeper—so deep that the cry of the psalmist, "Out of the depths, I cry to thee, O Lord!" rings terribly true (Psalm 130:1).

The pieces aren't yet all together for my friend. In a sense, they probably never will be because she cannot be who she was before the breakup.

Life has evolved from a salvage operation to growth, and that has been a struggle of joy. It has meant, more than anything else, a quest for stability, for the warm, dark soil needed for personal and spiritual growth.

With that priority, my friend has moved ahead to conquer bitterness and hatred and to build a life that moves beyond reacting in the present to residual pain from the past. Her children are raised by a mother who takes her baptismal vows and those she made for her children seriously, and the commitment shows.

There are certainly lessons to learn on a clinical level, things to be taken apart and examined. However, my friend's life is a testimony—a testimony to how God works in the life and struggle of a single mother. As such, it is a testimony of hope for all persons whose love is not returned and for whom the burden of emptiness is heavier than granite.

Rick Cartwright
Pennsylvania

Dealing with Anger

Anger is an emotion with which Christians often have difficulty. We're taught that anger is unacceptable, so we try to cover our feelings and hide behind a mask. If we go ahead and express anger, we feel a tremendous amount of guilt.

But anger is a very strong, very real part of our lives. It's *essential* in its proper place and perspective. We're all familiar with the anger that Christ experienced against the money changers in the temple. However, if anger is allowed to take over someone's life, it controls all of that life and consumes all the positive energy he or she has available.

Anyone who has experienced the loss of a loved one through death or divorce needs to go through the steps of grief. One step that cannot be avoided is anger. In many cases, it's the most difficult to work through.

In order to deal with anger, we need to know it's okay to be angry. Before we can go beyond anger, bitterness, and resentment to acceptance of the past, we must feel and express our anger.

Next, we have to forgive the ones at whom we're angry, especially ourselves. Others may have been unreasonable and unfair; however, in order to deal with anger, we must eventually forgive others.

Then, we must totally release our anger. Don't hang on to it—we must let it go. We can talk to friends and to God and ask them to help us release. Perhaps they can help us acknowledge why it is easier to remain angry than to give it up. Finally, we can ask God to help us replace the anger with forgiveness, joy, and peace.

Rita E. Yackley
North Carolina

Learning to Dance

All my life
I've been a dancer.

Yet for many years
The music was far away
Muffled—static
And I almost lost
The ribbon to lace my dancing shoes

So I had to break out
Get clear—
Free from the environment
That created the static
Distorting the reception

Now I am struggling
Learning new steps
Daring to create new movement
Dancing words on paper
Dancing with my body
Dancing deep in my soul

I dance
Not knowing how this dance will end . . .

Kathi Breazeale Finnell
California

For Healing

The sharing of pain
cannot always occur.
It is a gift of trust
that must be given freely, or not at all.

Those who are able to receive it
have done their own hurting
and healing
and so they recognize the signs.

It only shows
to those who have the experience
and do not reject it
but choose instead to live it through to the other
side.

Those who listen deeply
to their own true voice
are better able to hear
the words of others
to recognize the Self in all
and know there is no Other.

And this is for my healing
as well as yours:

Sometimes we do not recognize
our own cries for help.

Marilyn R. Pukkila
Maine

To Trust Him More

Dear God,

It's happened again! Another engagement announced in my singles group.

I want to be happy for them—these women are my friends and have longed to find someone special to share their lives with.

But, God, so have I! The jealousy, yes, even anger, is eating away at me, like a festering sore that refuses to heal, plummeting my self-esteem even lower. Oh, God, I'm so lonely. Why must I be a veteran in the singles' war?

I guess I already know the answer, don't I, Lord? You've shown me time and again through your word and your Spirit that my unhappiness is really lack of trust. Will you help me, Lord? Will you increase my faith that I might trust you more? Help me trust you with my life, with my future. Married or single— trust you to guide me into your perfect will where I can know peace, joy, and self-worth as a child of God.

Thank you, Lord, for hearing my prayer.

Nona M. Whitehead
Texas

Needs

I thought my marriage would last a lifetime, but
now I know what it's like to be single again: to be a
man eating out of a can, to be a woman broiling fish
in a microwave dish, to do a good job at work with no
support at home, to have others speak of my "freedom" as if all were sport, to plan for one when I'm
used to two, not to do many things that I used to do.

Family, I need closeness, support, and then some
    space.
Friends, I need a rational ear and also a word of truth
    in love.
Boss, I need time off to get together now and then.
Pastor, I need nourishment and encouragement
    from God's word.
Child, I need *your* patience for a change.
Lord, I need you near me all the time.

It's hard to walk or fit in my shoe,
unless perhaps it's happened to you,
especially for those of you who never knew
being alone.

Stephen K. Hoskins
Tennessee

A Place Within

Though its pathways be well hidden, I tell you now, I know of a special and sacred place within. The place is built on a foundation of love. The walls are crystal through which the light of truth dances in a kaleidoscope of colors. Shelves are filled with books of knowledge to comfort the generations. The place is warmed by the wisdom of the eternal and protected by the hand of the creator. In the darkness of its hallways glows the steady flame of hope. In the air, gentle waves of peace and tranquility rhythmically resound. Here is where I dwell. I am like the raven who would leave its nest to seek the treasures of the world beyond. I, too, venture outward where I gather the treasures I find and carry them back to decorate the place within.

Yet, it was not always so. There was a time when the innocence of youth allowed into the place those who would deface it with lust and avarice. Their roars of submission and denial broke the rhythm of peace and tranquility. The foundation was rocked by the quake of rejection and buried deep beneath mounds of broken dreams. The spirits of these roamed the hallways of darkness, and their laughter extinguished the flame of hope. By wings of terror, I flew from this place and hid, cold and afraid, in a distant and unfamiliar land.

In those days, the veil of death spread before me and tempted me to warm myself in its folds. Yet, as I knelt to lay down my weary soul, a voice spoke to me. It recalled the beauty once known in the place within. The voice offered to me keys of courage by which to unlock the doors of fear and strength of conviction with which I could defeat the apparitions of the past. So armed, I began my long journey back.

It came to pass that I reached again the place within. By the will of God and strength of conviction, I opened the doors and exorcised the spirits there. Banished were the roars and laughter that shattered the peace and tranquility. Lit again was the flame of hope. By its light, with tears of understanding, I cleansed from the walls the defecation which obliterated the beauty of truth. With a feather of patience, I swept from the foundation crumbled pieces of dreams and crushed essence of youth. I bathed in the warmth of wisdom and read again from the cherished books of knowledge. I knew the joy of the place within.

Never again, I vow, will I let another enter to defile the place within. Yet, I hear in that vow the echo of loneliness. There are still rooms and pleasures within that remain hidden behind locked doors . . . the keys to which are held by another and whose portals may only be crossed by the spirit of togetherness. I long for the time when I know of one who would draw from the foundation of love, comprehend the beauty of truth, and delight with me in the abundance of the place within.

Laurel Austin Hartwell
Pennsylvania

God is our refuge and strength,
  a very present help in trouble.
Therefore we will not fear though the earth should
  change,
    though the mountains shake in the heart of the sea;
though its waters roar and foam,
    though the mountains tremble with its tumult.

—Psalm 46:1-3

Beginning

Words of warning—
Actions of promise.

Drawn through pain and loneliness—
Torn by wounds that may never heal.

Vows of independence—
Feelings of obligation.

Protected by honesty—
Unarmed with a mending heart.

Cynthia Heidelberg
Nebraska

Suffering

One suffering face awakens in us the solemn memory of many who suffer. We remember the time we were in the hospital, the funeral we attended, those nights we couldn't sleep. We have vague recollections of half-naked children, bellies swollen with hunger; we remember the countless wars throughout our planet's history.

Our minds become a collage of words like *poverty, violence, death,* and *sorrow.* The images that accompany these words are always specific and individual: the knifing we witnessed in the street, a barefoot child with a dirty face, the loved one who went away. We do our best to deny that these images are real, but suffering and oppression continue to haunt us.

Jesus was no stranger to pain and suffering. Just as Jesus lived and suffered in our world, so God feels the essence of despair in each of us. Because God loves creation, we can experience with God the beauty of the morning light. Because God is within us, we can be arms enfolding each other in love, a love growing in strength with each added heart.

What can the old scholar of despair teach us about bodies swollen with hunger, drops of blood, or death in living? When we look with true caring upon the image of one suffering face, we must dare to dream amidst the raging pain of doubt and fear. We must look into the vague dark eyes of discontent and see the seeds of strength.

Blessed those who find their strength in you,
  whose hearts are set on pilgrimage.

As they pass through the Valley of the Balsam,
they make there a water-hole,

As they pass through the Valley of the Balsam,
they make there a water-hole,
and—a further blessing—early rain fills it.
They make their way from height to height.

—Psalm 84:5-7 (NJB)

Melissa J. Dudley
Texas

Mourning

Mourning is pain, tears, emptiness.
Grief shared in silence brings companionship that
   soothes the hurt.
Healing comes unexpressed and unexpected.
Eyes open.
The sun shines.
The heart sings!

Helen G. Hopkins
Pennsylvania

Blessed are those who mourn, for they shall be comforted.

—Matthew 5:4

Oh God!

How I shrink from the stench of death. Those cold memories freeze my very being. The smell of loss is all around me. How can I enter that place of death? How can I embrace those feelings associated with mourning? Oh, how I hate solemn assemblies gathered like vultures watching me emerge from the tomb of lost relationships and memories.

Yet, God, I know that through death comes life. You walked those halls of the tomb. You felt the bitterness of the loss of your beloved Son. *And,* you've taught us that life lives on the other side of death. So, God, walk with me. Guide me through these days of loss and mourning. Help me embrace the memories, and lead me into the light of promised new life.

Amen.

Karen Greenwaldt
Tennessee

"A Time to Keep, and a Time to Cast Away"

Looking Forward

Truly, I say to you, if you have faith as a grain of mustard seed, you will say to this mountain, "Move from here to there," and it will move; and nothing will be impossible to you.

—Matthew 17:20-21

Rebirth

Growth is a process of simultaneous deaths and births. Life requires that we let go of and give up parts of our being so we can reform, change and grow. Living must be a series of rebirths, particularly if we are Christians. The life of grace offers countless new beginnings.

Rebirths and new beginnings are often unnerving. They are times when we move into new areas and phases of living. Although it can be unsettling, I think this movement is a part of the abundant life about which Jesus spoke.

Over the past few months, new growths and experiences have been abundantly present in my life. If I had not been willing to let go and allow some deaths to occur, a new creation would not have been born within me.

Letting go of the past is difficult for me because a little of me goes with each part I let go. But many times it is in letting go that an event becomes reshaped, renewed, and reconnected to increase the quality of my life.

My assurance in this growth process comes from Paul's statement in Philippians 1:6: "He who began a good work in you will carry it on to completion until the day of Christ Jesus" (NIV).

Howard Harris
Oklahoma

Setting the Tone

1. How do I choose to handle the difficulties in my life? What skills and resources do I have?

2. How can I use my difficulties to help me grow into myself?

3. What in my life do I want to say no to? Old grievances, hurts, patterns of unhealthy responses? What am I ready to cast away?

4. What in my life do I want to say yes to? Solitude, friendship, forgiveness, a stronger relationship with God? What will I keep?

A Prayer

Father,
People speak of brokenness
 and being made whole again.
                              Again?
When was I ever whole?
As a child I was just beginning . . .
 growing, but incomplete,
    inexperienced,
        unwise,
            untried.
The young adult was busy with becoming
 dreaming,
    planning,
        building,
            working
                to achieve happy expectations.
But the years confounded the plans
 and disappointed the dreamer.
    Sorrow and pain defeated the worker
        and destroyed all that was built.
Brokenness I understand
 and I sort through the battered pieces
    to salvage enough to limp onward,
        away from the wreckage of depression.
But wholeness?
 I asked a wise lady,
 "Will it ever come,
 the day when all the pieces are put together again
    and I am complete?"
She answered,
 "The pieces will go back together again,
    but we are not complete until we die."

But do I want to be pasted together again
  like a complicated Humpty Dumpty?
    A cracked version of my former self?
Lord, help me rebuild a new me
  with understanding,
    compassion,
      fortitude,
        and gratitude,
As whole as I can be
  until my days are complete.

                              Amen.

Glenda Taylor Emigh
Pennsylvania

Choose Happiness

A number of years ago, I attended a weekend seminar. The leader began the first session by writing a sentence on the flip chart. "I can, by a decision of my will, change my state of being." That startled me. At first, I thought it couldn't be true because if it were we would all be happy all the time. Who wouldn't choose happiness over anger or sadness?

The next time I became angry, I did remember the statement and found out immediately it was true. I could *choose* to drop my anger. However, I was surprised to discover that I didn't want to—I wanted to stay angry. I felt justified in blaming the other person for my feelings.

I finally did decide to stop being angry. Then a strange thing happened, an unexpected bonus. I felt a new sense of power. I experienced a degree of control over my own life that I hadn't realized possible. I was no longer at the mercy of people who could "push my button." I could actually choose my state of being.

Through the years, there have been many opportunities to apply this idea. I've discovered that I can apply it to all emotions. I'm convinced that there are alternatives to fear, anger, or hurt feelings. We can't always choose our circumstances, but we can choose our responses. We can decide to have honest dialogue, to understand, to forgive, and to accept. It's this choice that determines our misery or our happiness.

Pixie Koestline Hammond
California

Lot's Wife

Genesis 19:26

You only paused but lost him
   down the curving road.
      You stood alone.

Why was it wrong to turn your eyes
   toward home where love had been
      and children born?

Was it so strange to feel
   the salt tears
      crystalize?

My love eludes me
   down the curving road.
      I stand alone.

Immobile for a time
   between the past
      and what will come.

Well meaning friends insist upon clichés.
   "Do not look back."
      "Life must go on."

The taste of salt
   is bitter
      on my tongue.

Doris Kerr Henke
Arizona

My Photograph

You think you know me—

You have only looked
    at the photograph,

There's more to me
    than apparent there.

The photograph was me
    for only a moment,

I still am—
    but you don't see that.

Julie Ann Manney
Florida

Storms of Life

When I was growing up in Florida, there were many night, afternoon, and morning showers. In fact, some months it seemed to rain at the same time each day.

I remember riding my bicycle home from fourth grade one afternoon. By pedalling as fast as I could, I stayed ahead of a rainstorm I could hear right behind me.

As I grew older, my mode of transportation changed from bike to car. I remember driving into a storm. My mother and I talked about pulling off the road to wait the storm out because its heavy rain reduced visibility. As we talked, I inched forward. After driving about thirty feet, we came out of the storm into bright sunshine. In the rearview mirror, I could still see the curtain of water. I wonder how long we would have sat by the side of the road if I had pulled off to wait out the storm.

Some of the storms in my life are like driving in the rain. I have a choice. I can pull off—pull out— and wait for it to be sunny again, or I can slow down and watch the guides in the road, moving slowly forward until I burst out of the storm into the light. When these storms happen, I have God's guidance to direct me through. The lines God provides along my highway of life come from the Bible, prayer, fellow travelers, and Jesus, who has traveled the road before me.

These things take time. We sometimes feel we're too busy and don't have the time for such things. I have to make adjustments in my schedule, such as getting up earlier and cutting some activities short- er, but I've also experienced the quality of time better spent. The storms of life are less likely to stop me or take me out of life.

One other thing I've learned is that Jesus would much rather take the storm out of me than me out of the storm. I like it best that way. How about you? We use up a lot of life sitting out the storms when we could be using the skills God equips us with prayerfully to move ahead.

Howard Harris
Oklahoma

Faltering First Steps

Faltering first steps.
Burned eggs.
No shower curtain.
Clothing chaos.
Strong needs to be
Alone.
Yet, longing for a call.
Any call.
But, I am learning—
Growing—
When all is said—
And done,
I expect to be better,
Stronger.

Asa Sparks
Alabama

Snowflakes

I walk briskly, aware of nothing other than softly falling snow and crystals, millions of them, gleaming on top of the snow-covered earth. It is good to think only of crystals and to look up into the sky and think only of stars. When I want to recall a scene of beauty, let this be it—stars and sparkling snow—crystals of heaven and earth.

I walk on and on. The rhythm overtakes the thoughts so that the rhythm itself becomes thought. No, not thought. It becomes spiritual—a meditation. That is how I survive.

I come to a fork and turn around. Homes are snuggled in the snow, lights beckon, and I feel the power of warmth and happiness and friends.

I walk over a bridge and hear the creek. It speaks to me of continuity, of the life-force itself, of water and people and their interdependence. Snow falls harder as I enter a small forest on the way home. Impulsively I sit down in the snow.

I remember a childhood—happy and full of winter days building snowpeople and making angels in the snow. I lie down and see only branches overhead; I could lie there forever and never move. No stress, no decisions, no pain. I escape for a moment. My life as a single parent presents so many challenges, so many decisions to handle alone. Snowflakes melt on my face and words of Dag Hammarskjold come to mind: "But at some moment I did answer Yes to someone or something and from that hour I was certain that existence is meaningful."

I wonder if I am saying Yes now when I so often want to shout No. I say Yes to now, but I know that tomorrow brings another day of stress. I am free of that burden now—surrounded by the gifts of trees and snow and night.

As I get up from my bed of snow, I feel the ocean inside me, surging, pulsing, with a knowledge of something greater than I.

I gather handfuls of snow and joyfully toss them into the sky and say Yes to now and everyday.

Marilyn Coleman
New York

Come to me, all who labor and are heavy laden, and I will give you rest. Take my yoke upon you, and learn from me; for I am gentle and lowly in heart, and you will find rest for your souls. For my yoke is easy, and my burden is light.

—*Matthew 11:28-30*

The River

A man was standing on the edge of a raging, roaring river that was filled with treacherous, slippery rocks. Lifting his eyes to heaven, he said aloud, "God, if you're up there and if you love me as you claim to, then you'll fly me over this horrible river so I can get to the other side and go on about my business."

Quietly, lovingly, gently, the Lord answered, "No, my child, I won't fly you over this river—you must go through it."

"No," cried the man, "I can't do that! Just look at those rocks! The water will smash me against them, and I'll be killed!"

But the Lord replied, "My child, you don't have to go alone. Take my hand. I'll cross it with you."

After I shared this story with a friend, she said, "You and I have already crossed all of our raging rivers. We'll never have to do that again."

She was wrong. As long as we live, each of us will encounter raging rivers—divorce, death, illness, loss, betrayal, heartbreak, loneliness, rejection.

In the last three years, I've realized that God doesn't bring these rivers into our lives. They come because we're human. But God's redemptive power transforms them into blessed experiences of God's unfailing and unconditional love.

But after each crossing, what then?

Perhaps at the next river, I'll stop shaking my fists at God. I'll no longer scream in the blackness of my despair, "Why are you allowing this to happen? You could have done something to stop it. Why do you hate me so? What are you punishing me for? Why, God, why? Why?"

Maybe then I can praise the Lord no matter what happens. Maybe in my midnights I can sing, "Bless the Lord, O my soul; . . . bless his holy name! Bless the Lord, O my soul, and forget not all his benefits" (Psalm 103:1-2). Maybe for me each day will be the day the Lord has made and I'll rejoice and be glad in it.

Perhaps at the next river, I'll let go of my anxiety and trust in the Lord with all my heart, instead of leaning on my own understanding. Maybe the fear that's held me prisoner will be conquered. "Fear not, for I am with you, be not dismayed, for I am your God; I will strengthen you, I will help you, I will uphold you" (Isa. 41:10). Maybe then I can unreservedly cast all my care on God, knowing that I'm cared for. Perhaps I'll hear with my heart, "I know the plans I have for you, . . . plans for welfare and not for evil" (Jer. 29:11), and I will commit my way to the Lord that my paths might be directed. When that river has been crossed, I'll know that I sought the Lord and was delivered from all my fears.

Perhaps at the next river, I'll forgive those who have rejected and betrayed me. When my rage, once kindled fiery hot against them, has been spent, I will wish them well. After I've hated them in the black secret place of my soul, I'll recognize that they, too, are beloved children of God, and I'll say to them, "I forgive you." In that I will be free.

Perhaps at the next river, I'll affirm that I am no exception to God's promise to forgive. Maybe I'll pray, "Create in me a clean heart, O God, and put a new and right spirit within me" (Psalm 51:10). I'll know God's truth, which will make me free from myself and from the terrible guilt that's kept me in bondage for so long. In accepting God's forgiveness and in forgiving myself, I will be made whole.

Perhaps at the next river, as I stand alone, I'll hear words beyond the roaring of the crashing water, "I will not fail you or forsake you. I have loved you with an everlasting love. Nothing will ever be able to separate you from that love. Love one another as I have loved you. (Jos. 1:5; Jer. 31:3; Rom. 8:39, TEV; John 15:12). Give to others the smile, the word of encouragement, the being there that is uniquely yours to give." I'll no longer be lonely.

Perhaps at the next river, I'll accept myself as the beautiful person I am, fearfully and wonderfully made a little lower than the angels, created in the very image of God. I'll rejoice in the miracle of me.

Perhaps at the next river, I'll turn and see you standing beside me, and I'll know by the look of pain in your eyes that you must cross this river too. Perhaps you'll let me take your hand and tell you that I love you. Then, perhaps you and I and God will cross that river together.

Vivian E. Smith
Kansas

In Process

By twist and pound
of curling wave
with salt, and ground
against the shore

by grit and wind
and sand refined—
from jagged rock
smooth pebbles born.

Creation's violence
shapes and molds
its creatures to
a higher end.

And I in struggle
scraped and worn
am polished by
my Maker's hand.

Marilyn R. Pukkila
Maine

Forgiveness

Forgiveness is giving up the right to retaliate. Forgiveness is the willingness to have something happen the way it happened. It's not true that you can't forgive something; it's a matter of the will, and you always have the choice. Forgiveness is never dependent on what the other person does or does not do; it is always under our control. Forgiveness is giving up the insistance on being understood. St. Paul said, "[Love] seeketh not her own" (2 Cor. 13:5, KJV). Jesus forgave those who crucified him. This is a radically new way of thinking. For those who accept and practice this discipline, there is a release of energy and a sense of freedom.

Create in me a clean heart, O God, and put a new and right spirit within me.

—*Psalm 51:10*

Pixie Koestline Hammond
California

Vision Therapy

Nine years and half a world ago, I went on a weekend retreat in an old convent in upstate New York. There were about twenty of us gathered around the fire on a cold winter afternoon, sharing our troubles—broken homes, broken hearts, broken spirits. We were wallowing in our mutual despair when the pastor interrupted us.

"You all sound miserable," he said, "and God didn't put you on earth to be miserable. Could any of this agony be your own fault?"

We were outraged. Bill had been laid off, Tom's son had been hospitalized for drug abuse, Susan's husband had left her. None of us had asked for these problems!

The pastor shook his head patiently. "No, but you've each made them the focus of your whole identity. Bill sees himself as Bill-the-Unemployed, Susan as Susan-the-Divorcee. You only see one side of the problem, so you only see one solution—and if that doesn't work out, you're lost. If you really are this unhappy, you must be seeing something wrong."

"Maybe we need vision therapy," somebody quipped.

"Maybe you do," said the pastor.

We considered this, and after a while we each shared the positive effects that could come out of our individual crises. Bill's job had grown stale years before the layoff, and this was the perfect opportunity for a total career change. Much of Susan's stress resulted from her frantic search for a man, any man, to replace the husband she'd lost; maybe she needed time out from dating to come to terms with herself. Tom's son's drug problems grew out of a longstanding wall father and son had erected between them, and perhaps this final cry for help could knock it down.

This, explained the pastor, is the secret of vision therapy. Most people accept depression as a normal part of life, the logical result of a hopeless situation. Because they only see one aspect of a problem, they believe that's the only view there is. Their <u>mental outlook is self-limiting, and their</u> possible solutions to the problem are limited as well.

Accept for a moment, however, the premise that depression is *abnormal*, that if you are depressed, you are seeing the situation incorrectly. Suddenly a whole range of options opens up to you. Not all of them will be equally practical, but at least you'll have several potential ways home. <u>The only difference between crisis and opportunity is the way you choose to look at it.</u> It's just a matter of vision.

Karen Livingston Raab
New York

Mental Health. Good.

+ Factors

Time

Change in lifestyle

Awareness of body

Self
Neck/Back
Prob

— Factors

Loss of health

Loss of work ability

Loss of physical strength

Loss of lifestyle

Pendulum

Choice of which way it swings.

Spring

I woke up this morning and heard a robin. It felt good, so I went outside. Walking in the yard, I saw a squirrel running through the trees, and I noticed crocuses starting to come up. I saw neighborhood kids for the first time in a long time. I saw a little mud in the house, and I gave a friendly reminder about a coat to my children.

All of these things seem different this year. Perhaps this life we lead goes in cycles. Maybe I will go out and play hide and seek in the neighbor's yard tomorrow. One thing I know this year, I am young again, and I will not let this beginning pass me by.

It is spring.

Bill Breitzig
West Virginia

Do not lay up for yourselves treasures on earth, where moth and rust consume and where thieves break in and steal, but lay up for yourselves treasures in heaven, where neither moth nor rust consumes and where thieves do not break in and steal.

For where your treasure is, there will be your heart also.

—*Matthew 6:19-21*

Almighty God,

It's so easy to stay put right where I am. Moving forward feels so scary. I know the familiar patterns of my life, yet there is something in me that wants to move, to shift, and to change. Could that feeling be you pushing me along? If so, where am I going, and why would you want me to go there? What do I leave behind, and what (and who) do I take with me?

I suppose I should trust that you know where I'm going, but sometimes it's hard to put that much trust in you. I've always heard "one step at a time." Maybe that's what you are saying too. If so, say it loud and clear! *And* assure me that you are going with me!!

Amen.

Karen Greenwaldt
Tennessee

"A Time to Keep Silence, and a Time to Speak"

Spiritual Growth

Make a joyful noise to the Lord, all the lands!
  Serve the Lord with gladness!
  Come into his presence with singing!

Know that the Lord is God!
  It is he that made us, and we are his;
  we are his people, and the sheep of his pasture.

Enter his gates with thanksgiving,
  and his courts with praise!
  Give thanks to him, bless his name!

For the Lord is good;
his steadfast love endures for ever,
and his faithfulness to all generations.

—Psalm 100

God's Presence Daily

Every one who asks receives, and he who seeks finds, and to him who knocks it will be opened.

—Matthew 7:8

Prayer has been called talking to God, and meditation, listening. We should give God equal time. A dictionary defines meditation as pondering or reflection on sacred matters. To meditate is to be on a passionate search for truth, not only about God but about ourselves and our environment. This is the search that brings us into awareness of the presence of God. It also brings all our relationships into correct alignment.

Just as in learning any other skill, regularity of time and place is helpful in meditating. I find morning time preferable. A place of quiet and beauty enhances efforts at meditation. Relaxation, correct breathing, good posture, and music may all be helpful, but the only essentials are a receptive attitude and concentration. I have a friend who meditates on the subway going to work! She has mastered the skill of concentration. Five minutes of focused time is better than thirty minutes of scattered mind wandering.

Most people are helped in going into meditation by some thought or statement. A scripture can help, such as, "My grace is sufficient for you" (2 Cor. 12:9). Perhaps a line from a poem or a song: "Breathe on me breath of God, Till I am wholly thine."

When pondering the statement's meaning, sometime in the stillness ask for direction, inspiration, oneness. It helps to have a notebook nearby to record ideas and guidance that may come. Many,

many times we may feel that nothing comes and no contact with God is made. Do not get discouraged. Guidance comes in varied ways. Maintain a spirit of goodwill and an attitude of receptivity. Answers may come later in the midst of other activities. Meditation time is never wasted. Skill comes with practice. Keep at it everlastingly. The time will come when we can fulfill St. Paul's directive: Pray without ceasing.

The goal of meditation is an expanded awareness, and every increment of new awareness is hard won and precious. The daily practice of meditation takes me briefly away from the busy world. When God is present in meditation, we are returned into the world strengthened, energized, and more able to love.

Pixie Koestline Hammond
California

Setting the Tone

1. When was the last time I dared to be silent before God? Do I fill my days with much speaking as a means of avoidance?

2. When was the last time I remained silent when I should have spoken? What do I need to do to have the courage to speak when words are important?

3. When I consider my own life with God, what do I see? What do I want to change? To add?

4. Am I willing patiently to seek God's guidance to discover the best life for me?

Metamorphosis

Swaying in the wind
Reaching out to God in me
Finding my center
Being called beyond my self

Sandra Mosley Gerhardt
Alabama

God Is

God is the one last try
Against never was and can't be.

God is the sunrise
The morning after
The day the dream died
And laughter was forgotten.

God is the tomorrow
In the today of dead love
And dying will.

Why is it
We never realize
Until our world is full
Of nothing
That God is all there is
And God is enough?

Roxi Pringle
Kansas

The Spirit too comes to help us in our weakness, for, when we do not know how to pray properly, then the Spirit personally makes our petitions for us in groans that cannot be put into words; and he who can see into all hearts knows what the Spirit means because the prayers that the Spirit makes for God's holy people are always in accordance with the mind of God.

—Romans 8:26-27 (NJB)

Focus

God is nearer to me
Than I am
To myself.

How I need
This moment
To pause and reflect
From my unceasing pacing.

Whirling, spinning, twirling.
Thoughts of the pressures
Of the week ended,
And of one coming
Kaleidoscope in.
Help me
To focus on thee,
The axis of my being.

Asa Sparks
Alabama

Seek to Find

You are not single-hearted—but whole-hearted
  For God is not far from every one of us.
You are not unaccompanied—but attached
  For God is not far from every one of us.
You are not going alone—but assisted
  For God is not far from every one of us.
You are not solitary—but integral
  For God is not far from every one of us.
You are not isolated—but sheltered
  For God is not far from every one of us.
You are not companionless—but beloved
  For God is not far from every one of us.
You are not separated—but connected
  For God is not far from every one of us.

Faye Field
Texas

I tell you, most solemnly,
unless a wheat grain falls on the ground and dies,
it remains only a single grain;
but if it dies,
it yields a rich harvest.
Anyone who loves his life loses it;
anyone who hates his life in this world
will keep it for the eternal life.

—John 12:24-25 *(JB)*

Closer Than Breath

And would you find God?
Then delve far into the depths
Of your own being.
Discover there
The mystery and glory
Of the Holy One.
Look no further
Than your own temple,
For the kingdom is within.
And in the sacred silence
Your Lord awaits your coming.

Pixie Koestline Hammond
California

Darkness of Fear

Beware the darkness of fear that would mask itself in the justification of need. See before you the shadow who would pretend to be your image. Is it not still the essence of darkness? So it is with need. Follow not your shadow, for it knows only the pathways of despair. Turn away from the guise of fear and behold the dawn of God within, in whose light the images of darkness cannot exist.

Laurel Austin Hartwell
Pennsylvania

My Comfort

My spirit cries within me,
"O God, I am your very child,
Abba, comfort me!"
I cannot see or touch your substance,
Just as I cannot see or touch the air,
Still I know that you are there.
You breathed on me and I took it in.
Because of you, I live.
Yet in the stillness as I wait,
My prayer is answered as I least suspect.
"Would you find what you are seeking?
Around you are my people,
Go, and comfort them."

Margaret Worman
Texas

Thoughts at the Grand Canyon

I stand upon the rim
and trace the layered aeons
rising from the canyon floor . . .
first the primordial fish,
amphibians, reptiles, birds,
and dinosaurs, until
time reaches me, an instant
in the cosmic plan.

Cool currents
of soundless air
rise from the depths
a swirling stream.
I am a grain of dust,
a speck floating in
the vast silence of eternity
and God.

Doris Kerr Henke
Arizona

Religion, of course, does bring large profits, but only to those who are content with what they have. We brought nothing into the world, and we can take nothing out of it; but as long as we have food and clothing, we shall be content with that. People who long to be rich are a prey to trial; they get trapped into all sorts of foolish and harmful ambitions which plunge people into ruin and destruction. "The love of money is the root of all evils" and there are some who, pursuing it, have wandered away from the faith and so given their souls any number of fatal wounds.

But, as someone dedicated to God, avoid all that. You must aim to be upright and religious, filled with faith and love, perseverance and gentleness.

—1 Timothy 6:6-11 (NJB)

Dear God,

I read these stories of losing, seeking, and finding. I realize that I am important to you—as important as a sheep, a coin, and one who returns from the far country. Your love is a searching love! Help me remember this as I seek you within myself and in relationships with others. Strengthen me to accept my losses, the things I do not find. Remind me that my honest seeking in faith will bring me closer to you.

Amen.

Kathi Breazeale Finnell
California

"A Time to Love, and a Time to Hate"

Love

Though I command languages both human and angelic—if I speak without love, I am no more than a gong booming or a cymbal clashing. And though I have the power of prophecy, to penetrate all mysteries and knowledge, and though I have all the faith necessary to move mountains—if I am without love, I am nothing. Though I should give away to the poor all that I possess, and even give up my body to be burned—if I am without love, it will do me no good whatever.

Love is always patient and kind; love is never jealous; love is not boastful or conceited, it is never rude and never seeks its own advantage, it does not take offence or store up grievances. Love does not rejoice at wrongdoing, but finds its joy in the truth. It is always ready to make allowances, to trust, to hope and to endure whatever comes. . . .

As it is, these remain: faith, hope and love, the three of them; and the greatest of them is love.

—*1 Corinthians 13:1-13 (NJB)*

To Dare

To know and let yourself be known,
To seek and search and explore in order to under-
stand,
To try and be the best that you can be,
To allow yourself to be pushed to grow,
To feel the hurt of another as if it were your own.
To risk the devastation of rejection,
To meet the challenge of being yourself and being
vulnerable,
To give of yourself more than you thought possible,
To share your hopes and dreams,
To expose your hurts and weaknesses and tears,
To be courageous in facing reality and truth.

So it is to dare to love and let yourself be loved.

Karen A. Foster
Illinois

Setting the Tone

1. Consider each line of the previous meditation separately, in reference to yourself. Is this quality of daring a strength or weakness for me?

2. Am I daring to love God, myself, and others? Am I daring to accept God's love? Am I daring to allow others to love me?

3. What can I do to exhibit a more loving spirit in my life?

To Be Made Whole

Love is when the other's safety, security, satisfaction, growth, and potential are as important and significant as one's own.

Love is potential seen and is not satisfied with less. It is woven well with tears, laced with anticipation—it is victory over fear.

Love is pain aching to be born from a thousand dyings, but it does not harm. It turns a potential for evil into creativity, a new origin—a well from which to draw freshness. It creates strength from weakness. It is the great equalizer of humanity. Love weaves together the accepted with the rejected, both within the self and between ourselves.

I love myself enough to be aware that all I judge wrong in other people are clues to what I reject in myself. Only then do I know that to walk with the town fool is to grace the hand of the King of kings.

Until that moment, peace remains a vision, a glimpse of what hope yearns for. Joy is the sensation of breaking through to that vision. It says, "Yes, there is the possibility of the dream becoming reality."

Until that moment, I fight relentlessly to give and receive all that I genuinely feel and sense.

I have learned to be real in my care.

I risk all that I can stand.

I strive to be honest in all its starkness.

I pray to walk gently, softly with my own soul and also with the spirit of another. For I know that I am on most holy and precious ground. It is God that I meet there.

Most of all, I remember that annihilation of another diminishes me.

This is not peace but war. The greatest battle is within myself. I resist being indifferent to the conflict, for it is apathy that numbs my soul, destroys my heart, and makes a mindless puppet of me.

I am not satisfied with less—less than what I know I can be, less than who I know I am.

Until that moment—
    When hope weaves with joy—
    War becomes peace—
Only then, does the raging storm become silent—
And wholeness tip-toes in unaware.

Judy Holleman
Virginia

Hold Them Gently

The incense curls softly
Around my face
Delighting my senses.
Yet when I reach
To catch an ascending wisp
It eludes me.

God is like this—
And love.
Do not clutch at them.
Nor reach to hold them in your hand.
Rather, be still and know
That they are yours.
And in the holy silence
Let their fragrance
Permeate your soul.

Pixie Koestline Hammond
California

If any one says, "I love God," and hates his brother, he is a liar; for he who does not love his brother whom he has seen, cannot love God whom he has not seen. And this commandment we have from him, that he who loves God should love his brother also.

—1 John 4:20-21

Commitment

I can never be
A whole person
Until I love myself
And equally
My brother/sister.
And that means
Commitment
To those I am
Close to.
And who I
Hope
Will love me
With the same
Heart of giving

Asa Sparks
Alabama

From The Heart

My heart says,
  "Please know me,"
    as I struggle with words
      to make myself understood.
My heart says,
  "Be my friend,"
    while I smile
      and try to win one back.
My heart says,
  "I'm hurting,"
    and I reach out in pain,
      and fear, and confusion for help.
My heart says,
  "Please love me,"
    but I am
      silent.

Glenda Taylor Emigh
Pennsylvania

On Knowing

Knowing you has meant an address
   a make of car
     a phone number
an interest in music, plays, dancing,
   or special education.

Loving you has meant a look in each
   other's eyes
     an arm around a shoulder
       a hug
a lent tissue to wipe away a tear
   a tone of voice.

Thankfully, I know you.
Gratefully, I love you.

David G. Broadbent
Florida

O that you would kiss me with the kisses of your
   mouth!
For your love is better than wine,
   your anointing oils are fragrant,
your name is oil poured out.

—The Song of Solomon 1:2-3

Your Friendship

You dared me to—
Risk life
Walk alone
Look up
Reach out
Seek Christ
Find myself
Smile
Pray
Know God
Love

Mary Lee Sonander
Ohio

Perspective

To love me
As you hope I'll be
Is fantasy.

To love me
As I used to be
Is memory.

To love me
As I am
Is love.

And God
does.

Shirley Gupton Lynn
Tennessee

Beloved, if God so loved us, we also ought to love one another. No man has ever seen God; if we love one another, God abides in us and his love is perfected in us.

By this we know that we abide in him and he in us, because he has given us of his own Spirit. And we have seen and testify that the Father has sent his Son as the Saviour of the world. Whoever confesses that Jesus is the Son of God, God abides in him, and he in God. So we know and believe the love God has for us. God is love, and he who abides in love abides in God, and God abides in him.

—1 John 4:11-16

Dear God who loves me as a father and as a mother,
    Give me the courage to dare to love through confrontation and vulnerability. Guide me with your wisdom to know when and how my love is needed—both for myself and for others.

Amen.

Kathi Breazeale Finnell
California

Karen Greenwaldt is Director of Single Adults Ministries for the United Methodist Church. She travels the country extensively to train leaders and encourage programs for the millions of single adults in our communities and congregations. She is a clergy member of the Central Texas Conference.